There are times in life when we find ourselves thrown back on God. This is particularly true when anxiety and insecurity overwhelm us. Connecting with God when our connectivity seems to have gone awry can appear to be adding pressure to pressure. But here is a book that reminds us that God's ability to connect with us never wavers. Tokunbo, an established Christian writer, well known to many of us, writes with real sensitivity and insight from his personal experience. Journey with him as he shows you afresh that God is mindful of you.

Dr. Hugh Osgood
President, Churches in Communities, UK

Although the subject of mental health has received diverse attention at higher institutions of learning worldwide, it is concerning that this is rarely the case amongst Christians, particularly in Africa, who are ever expected to live by faith, with all kinds of positive confessions. With this work, our brother has proved that the Lord is mighty to save a mind that is thus afflicted. From sharing his own experience, as well as expounding the experiences of notable 5-star Bible characters, Tokunbo has given us all, sufferers and their families, the opportunity to be open, sincere and hopeful in a God that wipes away every tear.

Dr. Ola Kris
Pretoria, South Africa

God is Mindful of You gently walks readers through a practical understanding of how God holds and guides us in our deepest struggles. Believers who have battled with severe depression or other mental illnesses often embrace lies concerning how God sees them. For me, this book does a wonderful job explaining that God is always with and at work in us during our most desperate times.

I see this being read *as a person goes through* their struggles. The exercises at the end of each chapter will not only allow readers to process their journey, but centre them in the presence of the Lord. Thank you for the opportunity to read yet another powerful book!

Apostle Theresa Harvard Johnson
The Scribal Conservatory Arts & Worship Centre, USA

God is Mindful of You is a masterpiece! Tokunbo eloquently describes the vulnerability all of us have to mental fatigue, burnout, and even depression. More importantly, he gives us a roadmap based on God's word, to breaking free and staying emotionally sound. I was blessed by the poignant and insightful lessons discussed on the importance of staying plugged-in to the presence of God through worship, prayer and praise, and how this helps us overcome the frequent drag effects that negative emotions can have on us all. To everyone who desires total life wellness, and to those who seek to provide support for loved ones, this book is a must-read. I highly recommend every invaluable nugget of truth discussed in it.

Rev. Kayode Tadese
Abundant Life International Church Commission, USA

GOD IS

MINDFUL

OF YOU

TOKUNBO EMMANUEL

SOPHOS
SB
BOOKS

CONTENTS

To
Destiny.
With Love.

FIRST WORD

MY STORY

AD 2020.

In the concluding chapter of my book, *The Shift of a Lifetime*, published in 2010, I had written about the year 2020 and the need to discover (or rediscover) a pathway towards significance.[1] Subsequently, within my circles, I began to emphasise the importance of the 2020 decade, in the context of personal and national transformation. Preparation was key. Big dreams were imperative.

On a personal level, the beginning of this new decade, the year 2020, was going to be huge for my family. My wife and I would both reach the jubilee age of fifty. My daughter would turn twenty-one, my first son eighteen and my youngest child ten. Talk about party galore! As well, my daughter would graduate from university and my son from college. More celebrations! To cap it all, we were to enter our year of milestone celebrations at the back of commemorating our 25th wedding anniversary in December 2019!

Suddenly, a few months before the end of 2019, the lights began to grow dim inside me. The small "fist of a man" in the sky of my heart rapidly became thick dark clouds of depression that threatened to pour torrents of doom and gloom. Passion dissipated. Vision was seriously impaired. Instead of looking forward, I was fixated on what was behind me. The more I looked, the less I saw of the future. I lost interest in the things that normally delighted me. I did not write, could hardly pray, did not run, and I went off social media. I was "away without leave" from the scribal community that I serve. I lost the motivation to service my publishing clients. I was in a deep hole, a mental abyss of some sort.

I had known bouts of depression for many years. On the morning I encountered God in August 1986, I announced to my mother that I had given my life to Christ. Her first comment to her teenage son was, "If you are born again, you would stop being moody." In other words, for her, the sign that I had gotten saved would be that I stopped being moody. Well, the joy of salvation certainly flooded my life that day, but, subsequently, the web of depression always seemed to find a way to spin itself around my soul. This time, just before AD 2020, it was a web of steel that clung to me; like those of a dark-souled spider man in a dark suit. There was no chance of me breaking free. Or so it seemed.

If there was anything that held me through those gloomy months, indeed years, it was the conviction that God was mindful of me; that His eyes were watching over me. Although I could not decipher, at times, whether I was cross with myself, my wife, my past or God, the knowledge that God was with me helped me retain some glimmer of hope in the midst of darkness.

This book is not about me or the details of my struggles. Its central focus is not so much on the *causes* or *triggers* of depression. Every person's story is different. And whilst it is beneficial to understand the whys behind depression (I tried hard to connect many dots during those introspective months), it is of utmost importance to know that God is mindful of anyone in a depressed state of mind. Not only is He mindful of us, He wants to manifest His power within us.

If you have grappled or are grappling with depression right now, this book is for you. Even if you are not one of the 1-in-4[2] four who suffer (or will suffer) from one form of mental health

problem or the other, you probably know someone who does (or who will). This book is for you
and for them. Surely, God is mindful of you.

#GODISMINDFULOFYOU

*Have you ever battled with mental health issues?
Have you had episodes of depression that seemed to
last and last? Are you struggling, even right now, to
cope with unfavourable circumstances and are constantly feeling anxious and fearful? Are you far gone
down the depression spiral and have experienced a
mental breakdown? I want you to know that, even in
your current situation, God is mindful of you. He has
promised never to leave you nor forsake you. As you
read this book, you will encounter the truth of God's
word and His awesome presence.*

HOW TO GET THE MOST FROM READING THIS BOOK

God has spoken once, twice I have heard this:
that power belongs to God.

(Psalm 62:11)

I recommend that you read this book *twice*. In the first instance, read it through, perhaps with a highlighter. Read with your heart and open your mind. God will surely meet you in this first reading. You will encounter God's truth and presence, and experience freedom in your soul.

At what point would this encounter happen? You would not know until you read through the entire book. It could be at the start, the middle or the somewhere close to the end. But you *will* encounter God. When you do, give Him glory and share your story.

Afterwards, read through *again*. This time with a Bible. I have deliberately referenced scriptures at the end of the book to aid the flow of the *first* reading. During this *second* read, you should open the Bible and check the references yourself. As you study and meditate on the word, the truths it contains will take firmer root in your heart.

You may want to do this second reading with a friend or study group. Ask someone you feel needs this message, to read along with you. Share your testimony with someone and embark on a journey of freedom together. Let the river of encouragement flow until it become a flood of immeasurable joy!

Happy reading!

1

THE COMING MINDEMIC

One day, many years ago, I climbed the stairs to the upper deck of a red London bus. Some people had already occupied the front seats, from where the view always seemed "better". I had to settle for a couple of rows behind this favourite space, on the left aisle. Instinctively, as humans normally do, I scanned the few people in front of me, not noting anything in particular. The bus was hardly full and everyone was keeping to themselves, enjoying the peaceful ride.

Suddenly, she began to talk. The lady who occupied the favoured space in front of me raised her voice. She was in conversation with herself or with someone in her head. I cannot recall a word of what she said, only the fact that she kept on talking until I reached my destination. The scene would stick with me for a long while.

I will never know this lady's full story, how she ended up suffering from schizophrenia.[1] What factor or combination of factors led to her mental health condition? Surely, there was a time when she was perfectly normal like everyone else, but somewhere down the line, life happened and she lost control of her mind.

Everyone has a history and life is happening around us everyday. Some are obviously coping well with the happenings of life and some are *appearing* to cope. But appearances can easily deceive. Underneath the made-up faces and well-ironed suits are souls at breaking point. Everyone is journeying along in communal "buses," conditioned to appear okay and look the part. People have learnt to mind their businesses in their minds, but often the mind is too full beyond healthy levels. If care is not taken, this peaceful bus ride may soon become an outbreak of hallucinating commentators!

Mental health problems, like depression, are often the resultant effect of unfavourable circumstances and the inability to bear their burden within. These circumstances can be sudden traumatic occurrences or protracted painful adversities. Instead of being upbeat about life, the person with mental health issues often lives under clouds of despair. Even when these break every now and again, letting in the warm rays of optimism, the darkness inevitably returns to bind the soul under shades of gloom. Over time, unaddressed *situational* depression can lead to *clinical* depression.[2]

THE PERFECT STORM

In the third chapter of *The Shift of a Lifetime*, I described the multi-faceted situation of an ageing cohort - Nigerians born between the years 1960 and 1970.[3] In 2010, they were in their forties and fifties; now they are in their fifties and sixties. Sixties and seventies are just around the bend. Of course, *ageing* is an inevitable fate of all mankind, but for those who were flung into diaspora wildernesses, and those struggling at home, there is more to it than meets the eye. The gradual fading away of long-held, euphoric dreams, coupled with an increase in stressful life events could lead to a mental health epidemic among this community.

Without repeating the issues covered in the aforementioned book, it is evident that debt, divorce, disillusionment and other disappointments will continue to cause different episodes of depression in people. Also, the tendency to "suffer in silence," more so because of upbringing and the stigmatisation of mental health problems, will only make matters worse. This deadly storm is rising.

What about Covid-19? Not many people saw this coming. But it is here, and most likely here to stay. Suddenly, life as it used to be in pre-Covid-19 days may never completely return. Thousands are mourning the death of loved ones. Drastic changes in social interaction customs are slowly becoming the norm. The economic impact will be enormous in the coming years. Already, millions have lost their jobs and the numbers will keep rising. Economic indicators are forecasting a global recession in the magnitude of the Depression of the 1930s. And if the past episode is anything to go by, the mental health spin off will be huge.

Another noteworthy point is what seems like a lack of preparedness among a generation of church-goers, especially African church-goers. Two or three decades of mainly God-wants-to-bless-you, expect-a-miracle messages, may leave the ardent believer confused about how to make sense of current developments. Why are all these "breakthrough teachings" not producing *break-throughs*? Where is the promised harvest from years of seed-sowing? Questions that were easily suppressed in the mind could begin to rise up and oppress the soul, leaving many severely wounded and depressed.

When all these and many other circumstances converge in one season of life - that is, sociological issues around ageing, adverse impacts of the global coronavirus outbreak, and the vulnerability of unprepared church-goers - a perfect storm of mental fragility is inevitable. This is the coming mindemic that could see all too many, like the woman on the bus, lose their mind and cast away every sense of self-composure.

#GodIsMindfulOfYou

Are you stuck in the valley of dry bones and cannot see any way things can turn around for you? Well, you do not have to figure it all out by yourself. The more you try in your own strength, the more despondent you would become. You should turn to God because He knows how to turn impossible situations around. Your condition is not hopeless. Your life is still redeemable. As you read on, you will encounter the Spirit of God breathing life into your spirit and causing what was once dry to spring with life and the brilliance of God's glory!

PRACTICAL TIPS

- *Identify and list the circumstances that trigger depressive moods within you. Is it your finances? Your relationship? Your career? Your dreams? Are you afraid of the future? Face the facts. When you find the courage to face your fears, they can become less intimidating.*

- *Be real about how the coronavirus pandemic has impacted you and may yet impact you in the future. Speak with someone about these issues. There might be practical help available with certain agencies that you are not aware of.*

- *Above all, be open to God. Do not hide your feelings from Him. Take a moment to pray right now. He cares for you.*

2

THE GOD WHO CARES
(Mark 4:35-41)

It is expected that waves will beat constantly against boats on the sea of human existence. After all, boats are designed to remain afloat, even when the waters are boisterous. But there are times when the storms of life threaten the survival of boats and their owners. In times like these, it really matters who is present in the boat.

Although Jesus promised to never forsake His own, feelings of being alone and forsaken are bound to rise to the surface when one is caught in the middle of a storm. Out of desperation and feeling helpless, we cry out to God. And all too often, the cry for help is, seemingly, met with cold silence. The only sound to be heard is the crashing of waves against the fragile boat, and the roaring of the wind in the thick of night.

Where is God when it hurts this much? Why does He allow storms to rage without mercy? Why do bad things happen to good people? Lots of questions. So few answers. In fact, no answers at all! Frustrated, afraid and annoyed, the person in the eye of the storm will soon give voice to his thoughts: "God does not care!" And it does not matter if it is the most religious amongst men.

This was exactly what happened to the disciples of Christ. They were all in a boat, journeying to the other side of the lake. Jesus was with them in the boat as well. They had not travelled too long when a furious squall arose and water began to splash into the boat. The more they tried to steady the boat, the more precarious their situation became. After a while, they wondered where Jesus was.

When the sailors on the way to Tarshish were suddenly faced with a life-or-death stormy situation, they all prayed to their gods and wondered why Jonah, the runaway prophet, was asleep in the storm.[1] Even atheists cry out to the god they do not know when their life is in danger. So, the desperate disciples besought Jesus, and when they found Him, He was peacefully asleep!

Why is it that, sometimes, the One who

promised to be close by feels so distant? How can the Lord who said He does not sleep or slumber seem to be unaware of danger coming our way? How should the religious person react when his God allows adversity to overwhelm his soul? The disciples did not hide their disappointment when they found Jesus sleeping nonchalantly in the midst of their life-threatening circumstances. They woke Him and bellowed, "Teacher, do You not care that we are perishing?"[2]

A thousand thoughts run through the mind of a depressed soul. "God does not care" is one of them. Or He does not care *enough*. If He cared, He would not allow circumstances to become intolerable. If He was aware, He would have done something already. If He had shown up when He was most needed, the situation would not be hopeless as it now is. Teacher, we are perishing and you do not care!

This is the voice of rock-bottom depression; the cry of desperation that is usually shrouded in silence and piety. There is no need to pretend before God. A sincere complaint before the King is better than a religious prayer full of hollow platitudes. He sees our thoughts from afar and hears the moans that we make inside. God would rather we express our deep thoughts to Him than stockpile them in a box of disappoint-

ment. The Psalms are relevant in every generation because they contain genuine prayers of
ordinary souls. Jesus quoted one of such prayers
on the cross when He cried, "'Eli, Eli, lama
sabachtani? that is, 'My God, my God, why have
you forsaken me?'"[3]

However, God cares. He does not forsake the
ones He loves in the middle of their troubles.
Even when it *feels* that way, He invites us to cast
our cares upon Him because He truly cares.[4]
God raised Jesus from the dead, showing that He
did not, for a moment, forsake Jesus on the cross.

When Jesus woke up from sleep, He rebuked
the storm that troubled His disciples, showing
that, even while asleep, He was always in full
control. The disciples were astonished at this
display of authority and they learned a precious
lesson that *faith* is a more powerful force than *fear*.

In the chapters that follow, I want to prove
from God's word, and beyond any doubt, that
God is mindful of us when we are battered by
life's circumstances and burdened by weights of
depression. It will become evident, I hope, that no
hole is too deep for Him to rescue us, and no
situation too hopeless for Him to turn around. He
cares enough to seek us out in our darkest
moments. When He finds us in despair, He is
powerful enough to restore our fortunes beyond
our wildest imagination. One moment, we are in

danger of being drowned by sorrow; the next we are safely on the other side of the lake of purpose. One moment we are in the depths of hell; the next we are revelling in the light of resurrection glory!

#GodIsMindfulOfYou

Have you been caught in the storm of life's tribulations? Are you wondering where God is or why He has allowed you to go through a season of pain? It is okay to express your heart to God. He invites you to cast your cares upon Him because He cares for you. He is there with you in the boat, even if it feels like He is asleep. The fact that He is in the boat with you is an assurance that you will outlast the storm. He cares. He is also more than able to calm the raging seas. Put your faith in God right now. He really does care for you.

PRACTICAL TIPS

♦ *Be open to God about the challenges you are passing through. Let Him know how you feel. Write a prayer in your journal.*

♦ *Be willing to accept the truth concerning how God feels about you and your circumstances. He cares for you irrespective of your current predicaments. Recall how He has helped you in the past.*

♦ *See the Lord rebuke the storms in your life. Visualise the calmness of the waves. Let the peace of God that passes all understanding flood your heart. Take a deep breath. Release all the worries. Say to yourself, "All shall be well."*

3

BEYOND THE STORM
(Mark 5:1-20)

⁓⁓⁓⁓⁓

Jesus had just finished an impactful teaching conference. The parable of the seed and the different types of grounds would leave even His disciples in deep thought. Who would want to be the person with a stony, shallow or thorn-filled heart?

Later in the evening, after a disciples-only question-and-answer session, and another general session, Jesus announced to the Twelve, "Let us go to the other side of the lake."[1] He did not tell them explicitly the nature of the mission beyond the lake, neither did He intimate them on what things would befall them on the way. The boat ride would soon get a bit rough because of a furious storm; the disciples would cry out in fear and Jesus would restore calm by rebuking the storm. This was the same boat journey discussed in the previous chapter. The disciples were oblivious to all these details.

I am always quick to say "Yes Lord" when He asks me to journey with Him "to the other side of the pond." But I wonder how willing I would be if Jesus told me about the storms I would encounter along the way or the enormity of the task ahead! When, in 2011, I uprooted my family from the comforts of London, UK, and relocated to the city of Ibadan, Nigeria, it was in response to a let-us-go-to-the-other-side instruction. Storms did rise and there were seasons of despair, but we also experienced the God who cares. In answer to our desperate cries, God rebuked the storms, calmed the sea and steadied our boat. Like the disciples, we learned that Jesus had authority over the storms of life. Beyond that, He wanted us to learn how to exercise the same authority over every stormy situation.

Back to Jesus and His disciples. After Jesus restored calmness to the waters and questioned the whereabouts of the disciples' faith, they all continued on their journey to the other side. Indeed, every adversity in life is an occasion that reveals the level of one's faith, and presents one with an opportunity to grow in faith. Even when the reaction to unfavourable circumstances is doubt followed by depression, the caring Christ is still committed to this progressive journey. He imparts valuable faith lessons of faith and leads us on beyond the raging storm.

If prior knowledge of an impending storm could have dented the resolve of the disciples to follow Jesus to the other side, what would have happened if they knew beforehand what or who they were going to meet beyond the storm? The main reason why Jesus left the successful teaching conference and ventured across the lake was to minister to a man in dire need. He was drawn towards the region of Gerasenes because of a man with serious mental problems.

Throughout the ministry of Jesus, there is ample evidence that He was always led by the Spirit and sought to do only what the Father wanted Him to do. He never journeyed purposelessly. Chances are, He knew about the demon-possessed man and went out of His way to set him free. In fact, the deliverance of this unknown man was the only event that happened at the other side of the lake.

Why did Jesus go to such a length to reach a disturbed outcast? Surely, because God was mindful of the man, even in his terrible state. But more so, because He did not see a hopeless situation; He saw a person who longed for freedom.

As Jesus approached, the man ran towards Him and worshipped Him. This initial reaction to the presence of Jesus revealed the desire of the real person, but there was a legion of demons inside him that had a stranglehold on his mind.

We do not know the man's background or how things developed to this state. But what we do know is that no one gave him any attention. The only way the Gadarenes, his community people, could deal with him was to bind him, chain him, shackle him and condemn him to life in a graveyard. In other words, to everyone else he was as good as dead. But not to Jesus.

Those who struggle with depression talk about battling "inner demons". They may very well be right. For some, depression is like a see-saw ride; on top one day, right down the other. For others, the battle is never evenly poised - one human spirit against a legion from hell. Thankfully, no amount of demons can prevail against the authority of Christ!

At what point did demons take hold of this man's mind? Was it a gradual descent into the tight claws of evil enabled by protracted engagements in diabolical practices? Was it a sudden traumatic experience that opened the door to these unwanted lodgers? Again, the details are not more important than the significant fact that Jesus cared enough to travel all the way for the man's deliverance. If demonic possession was the worst possible case of mental handicap, then Jesus proved that His love was more than able to connect with the lost man and free him from bondage.

After casting the demons out of the man, Jesus embraced him and confirmed him as a disciple. All the people from the region came to where they were and met the man "sitting at the feet of Jesus, clothed in his *right mind*."[2] As long as there is life, there is always hope. Life may be as horrid as hell, but there is hope still. The presence and intervention of Jesus can turn the ugliest situation around.

This Gadarene was worth all the trouble on the lake. He was worth more than a lucrative herd of pigs. Jesus transformed him from an outcast to an evangelist. The Gadarene evangelist would end up spreading the good news of Christ to the Decapolis—meaning ten cities.[3] What God has in store for you is a thousand times greater than your present predicament. He is mindful of you and of the destiny He has ordained for you.

#GodIsMindfulOfYou

God sees the heart you have to worship and serve Him. He also sees the chains that have kept you bound. In spite of all that you have gone through, you are still holding on. You are worth the journey over troubled waters. Your life is worth the sacrifice on the cross. Jesus draws near right now. His presence and His glory is flooding your heart. A legion of devils cannot withstand His ambience. A thousand chains cannot resist His power. The mountains quake before Him. The rivers part in two. You are freed from the pain you once knew. Your mind is completely restored. God is mindful of you. He will never abandon you in the graveyard of depression.

* * *

PRACTICAL TIPS

- *If you are suffering from any form of clinical depression, seek professional and medical help.*

- *No matter the severity of your condition, retain the hope of deliverance by stirring up your heart for worship. Listen to worship music and connect with God.*

- *Be open to prayer and deliverance. Call for elders in the faith to pray with you.*

4

GIVE ME A DRINK
(John 4:1-30)

⁂

The Gadarene deliverance was not a fluke. Jesus was intentional about His journey across the lake. He went to seek and save a man who had lost his mind. He would do the same for a woman who had lost all hope of a meaningful life.

Again, Jesus chose to leave what many would consider "ministry success." He had begun to baptise and make more disciples than John the Baptist, that even the Pharisees took notice. But Jesus, not at all interested in playing the numbers game, left the Judea region and decided to go back to Galilee, the place where He was baptised.[1]

Judea to Galilee was a northward journey, with Samaria situated in the middle. Normally, the devout Jew will travel the longer route to avoid contact with Samaritans. The roots of animosity between them went very deep. Who wants to relate (or be seen to be relating) with second-class, half-bred, worse-than-a-dog kind of people? Certainly not the lofty Jew of Jesus' day! But on this occasion, Jesus "needed to go through Samaria."[2] There was a needy woman of whom God was mindful.

It is bad enough for a person to continually carry the inner pain of prejudicial treatment just because his or her background is different from others. Even more damaging is the feeling of rejection when kindred people dish out the same kind of maltreatment. The person on the receiving end of societal stigmatisation sleeps and wakes in a constant state of despondency. The dark clouds of despair seem to always hang over the head, permanently blocking the rays of hope and acceptance from shining through.

We have come to know her as the "Samaritan" woman. Have we labelled her so because she was from downtown Samaria? Even her downtown neighbours avoided her like a plague. She had long decided to avoid any form of contact with them because they always turned their faces the other way when she showed up. To spare them the trouble, the "Samaritan" woman visited the well of Jacob at noonday, when the gossiping throng would be in the comforts of their homes.

Almost every sermon I have heard about this dear lady labelled her a prostitute. Where in the text was she described as such? How easy it is to place labels on people when we do not know their full story! Most of the time, the labels are false. Sadly, the stigma they generate has a way of sticking. If only we would, for a moment, put ourselves in other people's shoes!

Let us even assume that she was a prostitute. Is there not a real person behind the label? Deep within the soul of the so-called "prostitute" is a delighted child who, when growing up, wanted to be a nurse or a teacher or a businesswoman. No, the little girl did *not* dream of becoming a prostitute. Life happened to her, and the only escape route she could find out of her predicaments was the selling of her body for bread. Dreams long buried. The stigma fully embraced. She has to survive in a world full of cruel opportunists.

Jesus was never put off by the demeaning labels that society placed on people. He chose to relate with "sinners", "tax collectors" and yes, "prostitutes". He did not exclude them, but saw them as people who needed a friend.[3] In becoming their friend, He also became their Saviour -

in that order. So, even if she was a prostitute, Jesus would still have passed through Samaria for her.

But she was *not* a prostitute. She was a person living under an unyielding cloud of grief and depression, having been *married* to five different men. The joys of being in a loving, lasting relationship, it seemed, would never be hers. She might as well just sell herself for survival, and not just to anyone willing to pay; to one person without the strings of wedlock. The temporary respite she worked out for herself did not deal with the root of disappointment that haunted her daily. Neither did it help the stigma associated with her failed marriages. In today's world, one marriage breakdown is enough to earn one a negative social label. If people only knew the backstory![4]

So, God was mindful of this woman's misery. He was mindful of her buried dreams. He could also see what was not discernible with eyes of flesh; that the woman had a longing to worship the true God. Jesus had to respond. He had to ignore his disciples' preconceived opinions about Samaritans and women, and make the necessary journey through Samaria.

The way Jesus turned around the fortunes of this woman is instructive for anyone who wants to be used by God to help the depressed. First, and this we have already seen, He was committed to going all the way to reach the woman. Secondly, Jesus created a secure environment of comfort and confidentiality in which He could minister to the woman. He sent His disciples into the town to buy food so she would not feel intimidated in the midst of thirteen men.

Thirdly, Jesus initiated conversation with the woman. Having waited for her at the well of Jacob, He used a familiar theme to get the conversation going: "Give me a drink." If He did not start the chat, the woman would have drawn water from the well and left without even a greeting. She was that downcast in spirit. Jesus used the physical water as the starting point for discussion. But He knew that the woman would not give Him water to drink and could not offer any form of empathy or encouragement. She was empty inside, and you cannot give what you do not have.

Fourthly, Jesus disregarded her animosity. He was on a mission to shift the darkness that overwhelmed her soul and fill her emptiness with overflowing life. If He took her initial reactions personally, He would have missed the opportunity to reach the depths of her person.

Fifthly, Jesus, through wisdom, stirred her curiosity and desire. He gave her a hint of the possibilities of hope. "There is life beyond depression. You do not need to be confined to a monotonous life of drawing water at noonday. There is another way. A better way." To this suggestion, the woman at the well voiced her interest.

People who are depressed because of protracted adverse circumstances know the agony of short-lived hope. They are quick to discard any sense of optimism because the real issues will never go away. They protect themselves, then, by dumping the real issues in a dark corner of their soul, and avoiding them in conversation. But Jesus went there. He touched on her pertinent issue through the operation of the word of knowledge. He asked about her marriage.

The word of wisdom from Jesus, "Go, call your husband, and come here," took the woman to the heart of her matter. She could no longer hide. She confessed the truth about her situation and, perhaps, expected the usual condemnation. Jesus, however, was not condemnatory. In fact, He *commended* her honesty. "You are right when you say I have no husband." If Jesus had criticised her, she would have reverted into her shell and made it even more fortified.

But she did not retreat. She came out a bit more and expressed her desire for worship. The moment worship became the focal point of their discussion, her freedom was just round the corner. Although, worshipping God is one of the last things a depressed person wants to do, it is a sure antidote to being downcast and a sure means by which a person can be freed from the dungeon of despair.

Once again, Jesus demonstrated the loving care of God to this woman and transformed her into an instant evangelist who would tell the good news of Christ throughout Samaria.

#GodIsMindfulOfYou

No matter the stigma the world has placed on you, God is mindful of you. He created you and knows you better than anyone else. He knows your backstory and loves you all the same. God understands the pain and is drawing near to you with His healing balm. He is restoring your identity and removing the label of shame. Recognise the One before you, the One who is speaking to you. He is Jesus, the Christ, your Lord and Deliverer. Worship Him in Spirit and truth for this is the purpose of your existence. The burden is shifting. The yoke is being destroyed. You are free to enter the city without shame. Free to share your testimony to the world!

PRACTICAL TIPS

◆   *Do you know people who may feel stigmatised because of their marital status? Reach out to them with love and sincerity of heart. Be a confidential listening ear and do not judge.*

◆   *Do you feel stigmatised because of your peculiar past? Recognise and embrace any opportunity to open up to someone who shows genuine care. Your past need not hold you back any longer. Talking with someone who cares could be the start of a new beginning.*

◆   *What subjects stir your passion? What skills or potential would you like to develop? There is something inside you that can bless your world. Join a common-interest group and network with like-minded people. Come out of your shell and be free to explore the possibilities.*

5

WOULD YOU BE MADE WHOLE?

(John 5:1-15)

———～⚬✦⚬～———

Feasts and festivals are always a lively affair. People dress to impress and the aroma of food fills the air. Chatter and laughter is everywhere. No one wants the party to end... But, wait a minute. Something is not right. Where are the "marginalised" in the midst?

Jesus once attended such a festival of the Jews. He watched as the people joyfully consumed food and drink. But something was not right. He did not see any of His "friends" - the sick, the prostitutes and the "sinners". He could not find the side-lined and the disabled, the ones who normally do not get invited to festivals.

So, Jesus went for a walk. He had someone in mind on this festive Sabbath day. He wanted to demonstrate the love of God to someone who felt unloved. Before long, Jesus found the people He was eager to engage, congregated around a pool called Bethesda. Amongst this "great multitude of sick people, blind, lame, [and] paralysed," there was "a certain man who had an infirmity thirty-eight years." God was mindful of this man and wanted to demonstrate His love to him.

When an unfavourable condition, like an infirmity or a disability, persists for a long time, it tends to have visible psychological effects. Not too many are able to rise against these odds. There are stories of some who, in spite of their physical conditions, have performed great feats in life. These ones retained their sense of dignity, made use of their God-given abilities and continue to inspire generations with the success they achieved. But for every one who rises above their obvious limitations, there are hundreds who remain incapacitated by their conditions.

This was the kind of scenario that Jesus met at the pool of Bethesda. Every now and again, an angel came to stir the pool. Immediately after this angelic disturbance, the first person to jump into the waters would come out completely healed. This was a miracle for only one lucky person; the second or third person to enter the pool, no matter the severity or mildness of their condition, got nothing. How cruel this game of fastest-and-best!

After many failed attempts made by the man to be the first person to get into the pool, his mind began to accept the permanence of his condition. Each attempt narrowed any glimmer of hope, until there was only darkness, a night with no end. But Jesus stepped in!

Jesus, knowing that the man had been sick for a long time, asked a direct and closed question: "Do you want to be made well?" Answers to closed questions are normally single words - yes, no, maybe - but this man gave a long-winded answer: "Sir I have no one to put me into the pool when the water is stirred up; but while I am coming another steps down before me." This was not the answer Jesus was expecting. Instead of exclaiming, "Yes, I want to be made whole!" the man said, "I have no one to help me into the pool."

Generally, man-made religious or social systems are designed to open the door of success to only a few, usually one person at a time. Some get invited to feast at the top; others climb the ladder by sheer determination. The vast majority are meant to accept the status quo and make do with whatever trickles down the systemic pyramid. The journey to this so-called "top" is very steep, and all too many give up the quest even before they start. They conclude that they have "no one" to lend them a hand; "no one" to open the door of access to them, "no one" mindful enough to favour them. Thus, it gets very crowded at the bottom, and the vast majority learn to accept and adapt to a burdensome life of survival.

So, when presented with the idea of rising above societal limitations, the suggestion is processed through the mechanics of the limiting system. How can I succeed if I have no one? Who am I to arise if I have nothing? Why attempt to walk if I am a nobody?

It is self-defeating to harbour dreams of success and constantly engage in negative self-talk. The one will always cancel out the other. When man sacrifices his dreams on the altar of self-doubt manifesting itself as inner self-harm, adversity and failure perpetuates. This will only ultimately damage self-esteem and reduce the chances of realising dreams to nought. It is a vicious cycle that can last a lifetime if its root is not dealt with.

After thirty-eight years of rehearsing the I-have-no-one-I-am-no-one mantra, Jesus showed up and gave the man an empowering seven-word command: "Rise, take up your bed and walk." This instruction, with its three-fold activity prompt, was like a shock to his psyche; a divine jolt meant to quicken all his faculties! It was totally foreign to what he was used to for nearly four decades. He had lived within the confines of his circumstances and was now being provoked to think outside the box and step out of his comfort zone. Although he could not connect with the suggestion at first, he quit the excuses and acted on the impulse to rise up. Suddenly, his limbs got healed and he found himself doing what he never believed he could do: walk with *his own* feet. The intervention of Jesus had made him whole!

Evidently, when Jesus asked the man if he wanted to be made whole, He was not just focusing on the healing of his body. He was also interested in the restoration of the man's mind and heart. It has been proven that there is a connection between the heart, mind and body of man. As a man thinks, so he turns out to be.[1] Habitual negative thinking will result in a negative life. Bitterness, unforgiveness and malice also have adverse effects on the mind and body. Many medical conditions have their roots in thoughts piled up in the mind. So, wholeness to Jesus, was all-encompassing. It was not limited to what was visible to the naked eye.

For this reason, Jesus sought out the man a second time. The first encounter was a powerful, divine intervention that lifted the man out of his life-long predicament—the healing of his body. However, Jesus saw the need for a second encounter, one in which He would teach the man measures of prevention. Jesus wanted the healed man to understand the scope of his healing.

We will discuss some details of this second encounter with Jesus at the end of the book. For now, it is sufficient to know that God was mindful of the man at the pool of Bethesda.

#GodIsMindfulOfYou

Have you been suffering a protracted season of incapacity? Has your condition resulted in a low sense of self-worth? Have you given up trying to succeed and settled for a life of struggle and survival? Are your thoughts constantly negative and pessimistic? Hear the words of the Lord over you today: Rise, take up your bed and walk! There is power in this spoken command to elevate you beyond your present limitations. Do not think of your future in the light of your past. Get ready for a new beginning, one which the Lord has in store for you. God is mindful of you and the potential that resides within you. In spite of lost years, your gifts and talents are still within you, waiting for you to rise and activate their use. Rise, therefore, shine, for the glory of God rises upon you!

PRACTICAL TIPS

♦ *Take moments during your day to become more aware of your inner self-talk. What are you saying to yourself about yourself? Arrest any negative self-talk as you would an offender. Refuse to agree with the lies of the negative description. If, for instance, you catch yourself saying, "I am a nobody because…," arrest the thought. Do not agree with it. Replace negative self-talk with the very opposite, based on God's word. Declare, "I am loved by God. I am accepted in the beloved. I am the apple of God's eyes."*

♦ *Make a list of as many "I am" positive confessions you can draw out from God's word. Speak them aloud to yourself every day.*

♦ *Visualise yourself doing things you have not done in a long while. Actualise your vision by stepping out to do them. When last did you paint? Write? Travel? Study? It is not too late for you to pursue your dreams!*

6

DO YOU LOVE ME?
(John 21:1-19)

He was the outspoken one among the bunch. He sometimes spoke without thinking. That was just his temperamental make-up - always jovial; never short of words or ideas; the first to express his opinion about a matter. We are talking about Peter, the ex-fisherman who Jesus called to become a fisher of men.

Extroverts like Peter always appear to be confident, daring and full of life. Nothing seems to faze them. They enjoy being the life of the occasion, making sure there is no dull moment when in the midst of others. Well, such people never feel depressed, right? Nothing can be further from the truth. They may *appear* to always have it together, but appearances can easily deceive. Anyone, no matter the personality type, can suffer from depression. It is just that the extrovert knows how to *cover* his real feelings when in the midst of other people. He often *needs* to be with others and sometimes dreads the torture of aloneness. It could, indeed, be the case that introverts, by virtue of their introspective nature, are more prone to mind battles; but extroverts also have mental health concerns of their own. Underneath the self-confidence aura is a mental accident waiting to happen.

The answer for Peter lay in discovering that those who would come to Christ, and subsequently follow Him, must experience the death of self. Extroversion or introversion do not count before God, but a new life in Christ. Both personality types need to experience the transforming Grace of God for the fruit of the Spirit to blossom. If natural strengths are not put to death, self-confidence will be mistaken for faith, self-love would pass for the unconditional love of God, low self-esteem will camouflage as gentleness; indeed, self and not Spirit would be the driving force of one's Christian walk.

Jesus, however, knows what is in man. He knows how to guide His own to the place where they realise that without Him they can do nothing. Those who avoid this place of stripping and dying will never know true dependence on God. They will keep running on empty and never exchange their weakness for God's strength. It is the desire of Christ to help the believer, no matter his or her inherent, natural disposition, experience this dying to self. It is a Peniel-like encounter, the place where natural ability is laid down for the sake of divine destiny.[1] In this respect, every man's journey is different.

Jesus is committed to journeying with His own all the way to the place where purpose in Him is fulfilled. He will follow through with this pruning and purging process, no matter the pain, knowing the fullness of resurrection life that will consequently be released. At every opportunity, He will expose the unreliability of self-reliance and the wisdom of relying on God.

Christ's commitment to transform Peter from a self-reliant fisherman into a God-dependent fisher of men started at this very point of exposure of the limitations of human capability. Jesus had borrowed Peter's boat so He could teach the crowd from it. After the teaching session, He asked Peter to cast his nets into the water for a catch of fish. To which Peter explained that he and his fishing partners had tried to catch fish all night. However, having heard the earlier teaching of Jesus and now that Jesus had given the command, Peter was willing to cast *one* of his nets into the river. He had come to the end of himself and was willing to act on Jesus' command.[2]

The result was colossal! Peter and his friends caught such a large number of fish that their nets began to break! Peter learned that the upper limit of his experience and ability was the point where God's power began. And how limited was his expertise! Peter's sudden awareness of his littleness in comparison to Christ's awesomeness made him disqualify himself from being a disciple. But Jesus was encouraged to hear Peter describe himself as an unworthy sinner, for only those who come to such an awareness are truly worthy of following Him. "Do not be afraid. From now on you will catch men." With this destiny statement, Jesus communicated His intention to transform Peter into the person He was created to be.

On another day, after feeding more than five thousand people with five bread loaves and two fish, Jesus sent the disciples on a boat journey to "the other side" of the sea, while He dispersed the crowd. He also stayed back on the mountain to pray.

It was now evening time and the disciples were experiencing contrary winds in the middle of the sea (we now know that Jesus always has a lesson to impart in the midst of storms!). Suddenly, "in the fourth watch of the night" they caught a glimpse of something or someone moving towards the boat. The *thing* was scary because it looked like a ghost walking on the sea!

Sensing their fear, Jesus immediately said to His disciples, "Be of good cheer! It is I; do not be afraid."[3] But confident (or doubting) Peter said instinctively, "Lord, if it is You, command me to come to You on the water." Jesus, *fully aware of Peter's ongoing death process,* bid him to come.

Without giving any thought to his actions, Peter left his shuddering colleagues in the boat and stepped out unto the waves. One step. Two steps. Three steps. Peter was actually walking on water! Then reality hit him! He took his eyes off Jesus and considered the boisterous winds. At that moment, Peter began to sink. He cried out to Jesus and his Master reached out to save him. Once again, Peter learned that he cannot live the supernatural life by his own strength or ability.

In the course of time, and particularly as the death of Jesus drew near, Peter's fears resurfaced. But he was determined to overcome them by the sheer determination of human will. Speaking to all His disciples, Jesus said, "All of you will be made to stumble because of Me this night." To which Peter replied, "Even if all are made to stumble because of You, *I will never* be made to stumble."[4] This was the voice of self-reliance, overconfidence and arrogance. He did not need to presume what the others would do. By comparing himself with others, Peter was demonstrating the folly of leaning on uncrucified flesh.

So, addressing Peter directly, Jesus said, "Assuredly, I say to you that this night, before the rooster crows, you will deny Me three times."

Adamantly, Peter said to Him, "Even if I have to die with You, *I will not* deny You!" And he managed to influence the other disciples to make the same emotional declaration.

Peter did not have to wait for long before realising that he had come to an utter end of himself. Not only did he deny knowing Jesus, at the third instance, just as Jesus had predicted, "he began to curse and swear, saying, 'I do not know the Man!'"

At the moment, a rooster crowed.[5]

Peter, recalling the words of Jesus, "went out and wept bitterly." He became convicted and deeply regretful. He felt totally devastated for letting his Lord down at a crucial time of need. He realised, once again, how unworthy he was compared to the Lord's almightiness. He was a wretched sinner. Jesus was spotless.

Why are we considering Peter's up-and-down journey? Simply because everyone who would follow Christ will, inevitably, go through a similar process of coming to the end of self. Each person's path will be different depending on their peculiarities, but the goal is the same: to bring us through death unto life. At times, the aftereffect of this ongoing death process is feelings of depression, where a person is disappointed by his own failings. You want to stand; you believe you *can* stand; you vow to God that you *will* stand; yet you find yourself falling flat on your face every now and again. A blanket of hopelessness wraps itself around your soul; the shackles of guilt fastens around your ankles and wrists.

Neither extroversion or introversion is spared from the pain of crucifixion. Irrespective of the path a believer takes to get there, the soul will soon cry out: "O wretched man that I am! Who would deliver me from this body of death?"[6]

The comforting news is that, through this entire process, Jesus was mindful of Peter. Remember, He had stated His intention to fashion Peter into a fisher of men. Jesus was there for him in the middle of the sea; Jesus was not going to abandon Peter at the lowest point of his journey. In fact, prior to this denial episode, Jesus had said, "Simon, Simon! Indeed, Satan has asked for you, that he may sift you as wheat. But I have prayed for you, that your faith should not fail; *and when you have returned to Me,* strengthen your brethren."[7] What care! What love! Knowing the frailties of Peter and the battle over his destiny, Jesus, the compassionate High Priest, prayed for Peter ahead of his hour of need.

But how, after such failings, would Peter return to Christ and strengthen his brethren? How do you pick yourself up after falling so badly? Jesus may forgive, but how do you forgive yourself? It is, at times, easier to descend to the routines of a lowly past than to rise to the demands of a high calling. It is easier to live with guilt of yesterday's mistakes than to embrace Grace for tomorrow's mission. Peter, even after knowing that Jesus had risen from the dead, decided to go back to fishing. Being the leader that he was, he also influenced others to go fishing with him.

But through it all, Jesus was mindful of Peter.

Jesus performed a *déjà vu* miracle for Peter "at the Sea of Tiberias." Peter had quit his calling because he had come to the end of himself and considered himself not good enough. If he could not stand for Christ when he was so sure he could, what chance does he have now that he is not sure of anything other than fishing? Jesus was mindful of his struggles.

Once again, Peter and his colleagues, fishing all night, caught no fish. But come morning, there was Jesus, standing at the shore and calling out: "Children, have you any food?" He then instructed them to cast their net for a catch, and to their surprise, they caught a lot of fish, one hundred and fifty-three to be precise. Even with this, Peter was still drowning in remorse. It took John to whisper in his ears, "It is the Lord!"

When they finally managed to drag the net of fish to shore, they found a coal of fire already lit. Jesus did not condemn His disciples. Instead, He asked for some of the fish they caught and prepared breakfast for them. No one uttered a word.

All this, really, was for Peter. So, Jesus took him aside and asked a compelling question: "Simon, son of Jonah, do you love me?" Why would Jesus ask such a question from a man who was reeling in guilt? Was He trying to pile more guilt on an already beaten man? Surely not. The question was not, "Why did you deny me?" It was, "Do you love me?" With this question, Jesus unveiled to Peter's heart what Peter could not admit to himself: that he deeply loved the Lord but his human, natural love was not sufficient enough to love Him. The three times Jesus asked the question was followed with a recommissioning to the calling to feed the sheep of Christ. Each question healed the pain of denial. Peter's life would never remain the same again.

#GodIsMindfulOfYou

Christ is committed to your destiny, but He cannot allow you to side-step the journey to the cross. The ups and downs of your walk with God are not enough reason for God to forsake you. He will never forsake you. He will see His work through in you. He is calling you back to the place of devotion. He is restoring you to your first love. Turn around now and do the things that you did in the past. Let go of regret. Forgive yourself of your failings. God is not mad at you. He is mindful of you!

PRACTICAL TIPS

♦ *Are you working on a project? Allow yourself to be a recipient of other people's help. You do not have to do everything by yourself. Receiving help is not a sign of weakness. Ask for help.*

♦ *Recognise the gifts and abilities of your partners and colleagues. They can complement you as much as you can complement them. There's no need for competition. Let your colleagues know you appreciate their particular gifting and what they bring to your joint endeavours.*

♦ *Do not quit because of failure. Talk to a mentor about times you have fallen short. Usually, mentors will have perspectives that you can learn from. You may have failed in the past. It is only an event. It is not what defines you. Learn and move on.*

7

ALONG THE EMMAUS ROAD
(Luke 24:13-35)

It was resurrection morning. Some of the women had encountered angels at the empty tomb, and broken the news to the other disciples. Peter and John had run frantically to the tomb and found it empty, just as the women had reported. What was the meaning of all these developments?

Prior to Jesus' crucifixion, the disciples were expecting the liberation of Israel from Roman rule. But their expectations were dashed when the One in whom they had hinged their hopes died shamefully on the rubbish heap of Golgotha. Although Jesus, many times, had made predictions about His death and the resurrection that would follow, the breaking news of an empty tomb did not immediately fill the disciples with delight. Instead, their hearts got flooded with dread emanating from unbelief.

When the believer's earnest prayers are not answered at the time and in the manner he expects, how should he react? When circumstances play out contrary to how the mind had worked them out, does it mean God is not at work? When heaven seems silent, does it mean God does not care? All these concerns can easily cloud the mind and drag a person into a state of confusion and depression.

When we make requests to God, He *always* hears us.[1] He is never uninterested in our pleas. Besides, He *always* answers. What we are not always able to discern is the fullness of what His answer entails.

God always *hears* and He always *answers*. His answer to any request could be, "Yes, right now," "Yes, but not yet," "Yes, soon after this," or "Yes, but not like that." God could also say, "No, not at all," "No, because of this," or "No, you really don't want that." When we lay hold of God's promises in prayer, God's answer is always "Yes."[2] But when we focus on things outside His will, His answer is often "No".

It requires *faith* to know that God always

hears us, and *trust* to accept the answer He gives. Without faith and trust in God, we would be prone to feelings of dejection because of the perception that our expectations have fallen flat. And when a person is downcast because of deflated expectations, it is not always easy to lift oneself up. Differed hope sickens the heart.[3]

The situation can only get worse when a dispirited person buddies up with another dispirited person. Instead of encouraging one another's faith, they get deeper into despair by affirming one another's unbelief. Iron can no longer sharpen iron because both irons have lost their cutting edge! Those who have thus lost their spiritual sharpness, get tempted to distance themselves from those who retain hope in spite of uncertain circumstances. They wonder how one could be thankful in adversity and conclude that others just do not understand.

This is why some are tempted to leave the congregation when they are passing through tough times. What they really need is an atmosphere of faith, but it may seem daunting to retain optimism when the spirit is bruised and flat.

So, back to resurrection morning. The breaking news of the risen Christ, which was the answer of God to the question of sin and death, was met with astonishment and unbelief. Many had not gotten over their disappointment at what they regarded as the Messiah's failed mission, and now an empty tomb! All this was too much for the discouraged Cleopas and his equally-discouraged friend. They both decided to leave the congregation in Jerusalem and travel seven miles to "a village called Emmaus."

Usually, a person who is feeling depressed wants to avoid interacting with others. They do not have the energy for positive talk. If they do get talking with someone, it is usually with a person with a similar low energy status. Adding two negatives only compounds the negativity. A depressed person cannot lift up another depressed person. It takes someone with a different outlook to help someone who is downcast. Indeed, Jesus had to reach out to these two friends before they travelled too far away from their destined place. He was mindful of them even in their state of despair.

These two disciples did not recognise Jesus at first. Their hearts were so dulled by sorrow and disappointment. Their defeatist attitude about the death of Jesus only made them sadder and sadder. They needed a different perspective.

When discussions are based mainly on human viewpoints or personal biases, it becomes easy to stray from the truth. But when Christ, who is the Word, is at the centre of discussion, the Holy Spirit is able to encourage and give life. So, Jesus stirred the conversation towards the revelation of Himself in the Word. The glow of His presence and the truth He shared changed the atmosphere around their hearts.

Even with this, they still continued on the journey *away* from Jerusalem. When they got to the village of Emmaus, Jesus acted as if He was travelling further, but they persuaded Him to stay with them. They now desired the company of a person full of hope and truth. The weight of depression had lifted. Their minds were now free.

At the table, Jesus broke bread, gave thanks to God and handed the bread to the uplifted friends. At that moment, their eyes opened and Jesus disappeared from their sight. Astonished and overjoyed, they journeyed back to Jerusalem and broke the good news to the rest of the disciples. Jesus is risen indeed!

#GODISMINDFULOFYOU

Are you travelling a path away from your purpose and destiny? Are you discouraged to the point of avoiding fellowship with others? Is your mind over-worked trying to make sense of what is happening around you? Jesus is mindful of you and wants to refocus your mind on the truth of His word. The answers you need are in the word of God, brought to life by the Holy Spirit, your faithful Teacher. He draws near now to open your eyes to wonderful things that are sure and true. Feel the warmth of His presence stir your heart. Catch the fire of revival and be restored to your place within the congregation. God is in control of the things you cannot control. He will never fail even when the systems of the world fail. Renew your mind right now and embrace Jesus, your Lord.

* * *

PRACTICAL TIPS

♦ *Talk about your disappointments and unanswered prayers with someone who, perhaps, may offer a different perspective.*

♦ *If God is always working things out for our good, ask the question, what might God be doing in this situation that I am not aware of? Explore this with a trusted friend who could also encourage you in the word.*

♦ *Talk with the leadership of your congregation if you are considering taking time off from the congregation. Be open to the fact that the decision to leave might not be the best. God can turn things around in an instant and change the narrative of your circumstances.*

8

OUT OF THE CAVE
(1 Kings 19:1-18)

⁓

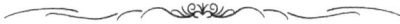

He had just finished confronting the enemies of God. Single-handedly. Although outnumbered 450-to-1, he was still a majority because he was on God's side. Knowing the futility of idols and the ability of God, he challenged the prophets of Baal to a prayer contest - winner takes all. His God against theirs. His supplication versus theirs. He and the God of Israel won in style and he took all the spoils - the lives of 450 Baal seers slaughtered at Brook Kishon.[1]

He was not done yet. With confidence beaming all over, he announced to King Ahab, "Get ready, it is going to rain!" Although it had not rained in three years, God had told him the rains were on the way. So, full of faith, he went on to the top of Mount Carmel to pray. Seven times he prayed until the clouds became grey.[2]

Hats off for Elijah the Tishbite, prophet of the living God!

Now, men and women of God are not susceptible to depression, are they? What can disturb a prophet who is able to survive famines, multiply flour, call down fire from heaven, and outrun horses? Who can possibly pose a threat to a prophet of Elijah's calibre?

Welcome Jezebel, daughter of Ethbaal!

It is erroneous to think that some people are too big to suffer from depression. In many cases, the bigger the status, the deeper the fall. Preachers, celebrities, public figures; they all have down days, even if they appear to be immune. For such, and for all, it is written: "Let him who thinks he stands take heed lest he fall."[3]

It is also important to be aware of the probability of falling soon after a great victory. After exerting energy to accomplish a feat, one may become tired and vulnerable, increasing the chances of burnout. The busier a person is, the greater the need for recreation and rest. Some just keep going as if they are super beings and not humans. The mind can be most vulnerable when the body is fatigued.

So, Jezebel only needed to send a threatening message to Elijah. Instead of countering the threat with confident silence or a much bigger threat (like his forefather David did against Goliath[4]), what did mighty prophet Elijah do? He ran for his life! Elijah "saw" what Jezebel said and fled! Not only did Elijah flee, he abandoned his servant who could have been a source of encouragement and fled some more.

Why did Jezebel's words have such a torturous impact on Elijah? Perhaps this is not the right question. Why did Elijah run away when he could pray? This may not be the right question either. Irrespective of the reasons for his reaction or lack of action, what was important at this moment was that Elijah was descending speedily into a pit of despair. After a day and a night of running, "he sat down under a broom tree" and wished for death. He did not attempt taking his life by himself; He asked God to do it for him! With a ring of exhaustion in his voice, Elijah prayed: "It is enough! Now, Lord, take my life, for I am no better than my fathers!"

God *heard* the prayer, but His silent answer was a "No, not at all!" How often do we pray for things we do not really want and wonder why God is not answering our prayer? Instead of striking Elijah dead with a thunderbolt, God sent the sleeping prophet "a cake baked on coals and a jar of water." What we *want* and what we *need* are two different things entirely. After tireless running, Elijah needed food, not death. Elijah woke up, ate the food, and went back to sleep. Sometimes when people are depressed, all they feel like doing is eat and sleep!

For a second time, the angel of God brought food to Elijah, woke him up and asked him to eat. Elijah needed not a single dose, but a double dose of encouragement! God will never give up loving and caring, even when the beloved has long given up responding to His care.

Infused with divine energy, Elijah ran for forty days, *not* towards the one who sought his life, but further away from her. He did not confront his problem, but was eager to avoid it. Truth is, Elijah was not running away from a wicked queen; he was running away from himself. He had gotten into a mindset that was out of sync with God's. And the more he tried to make sense of his circumstance from that inner, faulty stance, he only ended up in greater despair. God wanted Elijah on the platform of his holy call, but the exhausted prophet sought comfort in a cave on the holy mountain of Horeb!

What was this misalignment that caused Elijah to resign his prophetic calling? Why was it difficult for him to snap out of the mental struggles he was dealing with? Each time God tried to engage and encourage him, the misconception kept oozing from the tired prophet. Elijah's conflicting view of his situation was that he was the only one zealous for God; the only one willing to engage in this seemingly unwinnable war against Baalism.

"What are you doing here in the cave, Elijah?" God had asked His prophet.

"Running for my life! This fight of faith is impossible! Killing 450 prophets of Baal is like snipping branches and leaving the root intact. I cannot win this war!" Elijah ranted.

God did not respond to Elijah's murmurings. Instead He told Elijah to come out of the cave and "stand on the mountain before the Lord." Now, this "mountain before the Lord" is the same mountain where Moses had an intimate God-encounter; the same mount Horeb where God showed His glory to Moses, causing "all His glory" to pass before him.[5] This was a mountain of intercession and transformation, a place where God wanted to reveal Himself afresh to Elijah.

The exhausted prophet was *ordered* to come out of the cave, stand probably in the same place where Moses stood centuries back, and partake of the glory of God. But Elijah, it seems, stayed back in the cave. Overlooking Elijah's slowness to obey, "the Lord passed by." And each time He passed by, there was an immediate physical impact. Strong winds blew, breaking rocks and rooting out trees; an earthquake shook the foundation of the mountain; fire fell from heaven and consumed all in its path. But in spite of these manifestations, "the Lord was *not* in the wind… the Lord was *not* in the earthquake… the Lord was *not* in the fire."

How can the Lord pass by and yet the Lord was not there? This is such a pertinent thought. Many times we want God to show up and change our circumstances, but God may not be in the change we crave. There are those who earnestly pray for God to slay their enemies. Even if the enemies die, does it mean that God was in the slaying? Some would do anything for a breakthrough, but does that mean God was in the breakthrough? When supposed miracles leave people unchanged in heart, we must question whether God was in the miracles!

Elijah recognised the "emptiness" of these manifestations and stayed in the cave. However, after all these, he heard "a still small voice," at which "he wrapped his face in his mantle and went out and stood in the entrance of the cave." Elijah was meant to come out of the cave and stand before the Lord on the mountain. But he was so out of sync that he remained sheepishly at the cave's entrance. When God asked him the same question that He had asked before, Elijah gave the same response from his limited, self-focused view point. Misapplied zeal. Misplaced trust. Mistaken observation. Misjudged conclusion. Everything goes amiss when one's heart is out of sync with God.

From that moment, the discouraged prophet became a resigned prophet; he would no longer take part in ridding the land of Israel of the worship of Baal. In his place would arise Elisha, Jehu and Hazael, who would take over from where he quit.

"And just for the records," God seemed to say to His beloved prophet, "I have reserved seven thousand in Israel, all whose knees have not bowed to Baal, and every mouth that has not kissed him." So, all this while that Elijah was feeling exhausted and wallowing in self-pity, thinking he was the only one standing against Baalism, God had seven-thousand others who had kept themselves pure from the spiritual infection. Elijah only saw himself; he did not see the *bigger picture*.

Truth is, Elijah could have recognised that he was *not* alone in the war against Jezebel. Before he revealed himself to king Ahab by the word of the Lord, Elijah met Obadiah, the man in charge of Ahab's house. You would have thought that everyone serving in the king's palace was eating from Jezebel's table, but not Obadiah. Even in the king's house, God had a witness. Obadiah had told Elijah how he saved one hundred prophets from Jezebel's clutches, hid them in two caves and fed them with bread.[6] So, even if Elijah did not know by revelation that there were seven thousand holy remnants in the land, he should have known by *information* that there were, at least, one hundred and one. He saw only himself and consciously chose the path of resignation and depression.

It is a dangerous thing to choose *not* to see what God is showing. God will reach out to the downcast with encouragement, but the discouraged would have to *receive* the encouragement for it to have an effect. God will not force encouragement on us. He will paint a picture of a broader horizon, but the low in spirit will have to raise their sight to see it. Until one decides to see prevailing circumstances from God's exalted perspective, depression can persist for a season.

Elijah the loner, always strong in his single-mindedness, had become Elijah the lonely. God had to challenge his self-pity and isolationism at Horeb, but God's mindfulness did not stop there. He revealed to Elijah that the battle to rid Israel of Baal would ultimately be won. Besides, Elijah still had a vital part to play. It was not time for him to retire. He may no longer be the one putting false prophets to the sword; he had done his fair share. But, as an elder prophet, he would raise and anoint the younger generation: "Hazael as king over Syria... Jehu the son of Nimshi as king over Israel. And Elisha the son of Shaphat of Abel Meholah... as prophet" in his place.

Elijah, equipped with a broader view of the big picture, "found Elisha" and took him under his wings. It might not always have been easy for Elisha once God placed him alongside Elijah, but he proved to be a kindly and determined companion right through to the moment when Elijah was carried up to heaven. Such is the extent of God's care for us!

#GodIsMindfulOfYou

Have you experienced victories in your walk with God, but have now suddenly slumped to the depths of despair? Are you tired of standing in faith and would rather run away and hide? Have you suffered loss and are finding it difficult to receive comfort from God? Have you wished for life to end? God is mindful of you. He has not forgotten your past labours of love and wants to assure you that He is in control of every situation you currently face. Arise now and stand before the Lord your God. His presence is with you; His still small voice is speaking comfort into you, imparting an understanding of the bigger picture. God has not finished with you yet. There are still more lands to conquer; more ground to cover. It is not by might or power. By His Spirit you will yet accomplish great things. The coming generation have a lot to receive from you – wisdom, experience and godly counsel. Arise and return. God is mindful of you!

* * *

PRACTICAL TIPS

♦ *When last did you take time to rest. Book a holiday for yourself. Others can take care of the work.*

♦ *Network with people of like passion with you. Share your knowledge and learn from the perspectives of others too.*

♦ *Start a programme to mentor the coming generation. Your legacy does not have to end with what you achieve; it should extend to what others will accomplish because of what they learn from you.*

9

ENTER THE SANCTUARY
(Psalm 73:1-28)

⁘

It is clear beyond doubt that God is mindful of His own. He will go to any extent to reach out to those who are oppressed in their mind. He may have ninety-nine who need no physician, but is deeply mindful of the one that is struggling.

God is willing to cross troubled lakes to reach one mentally ill person, journey through forsaken regions to touch one stigmatised woman, leave happy feasts to heal one disabled person, focus intently on restoring a dejected disciple, and travel seven miles to restore a pair of confused friends. He would even go all out to revive a discouraged prophet. In all these instances, God took the initiative to reach out to the afflicted in soul. His glorious presence touched their hearts and restored their minds. His truth set a new course for the freed person. Depression cannot persist when a heart is stirred by the love of God and a mind illuminated by His truth! In the presence of Jesus is fullness of joy![1] Embracing His truth is key to lasting freedom![2]

Again, when a depressed soul encounters the presence and truths of God, the circumstances that triggered the depression fade into oblivion. The chains that bound the mind shatter into many pieces. The dark clouds that engulfed the heart are blown away. The spirit of heaviness is swapped for the garment of praise.[3] O for the presence of God that sets the lawful captives free!

Coming into the presence of God was important to David. As a young shepherd boy, he had gotten accustomed to the presence of God, worshipping as he cared for sheep. Later, while serving King Saul, he had found that playing his harp could create such a sense of God's presence that calmed the seriously troubled king.[4] When he became King, David was never slow to bring his own troubles into God's presence. He also encouraged the psalmists he gathered around him to do the same. He taught them the secret of defeating depression no matter the prevailing circumstance: *trusting God's truth enough to activate His presence through worship.*

Your soul may become downcast, but you do not need to remain depressed if you enter God's presence and engage Him through worship. This is one of the underlying messages from the Psalms, and the reason why they are loved the world over. We identify with the psalmists as they express their feelings before the Lord. Even Jesus used a Psalm of David, the twenty-second Psalm, to express His anguish on the cross: "My God, my God, why have you forsaken me?"[5]

If you look closely, however, what may have started as a heartfelt cry of desperation and a description of utter despair, soon ends in an outburst of praise to God. In the same song, you witness the interaction between a heavy-hearted songwriter and his all-powerful God, who is worthy of praise. The psalmist feels the pain of his circumstances but also acknowledges the comfort of his Maker.

The twenty-second Psalm that Jesus recited started with a cry of dejection, but ended with a prophetic declaration of the praise of God reaching "the ends of the earth."[6] How can a lamentation triggered by oppressing circumstances switch half-way through and become an expression of praise to God? The secret is that the lamentation was sung *before* God, as a prayer *to* Him. Also, the psalmist's outward pain did not overshadow his inward trust in God. While the pain was a present reality, the faithfulness of God in times past inspired trust and shaped the outlook of the future. In expressing his feeling directly to God and retaining the notion of God's trustworthiness, the psalmist experienced breakthroughs within and without.

So, in this twenty-second Psalm, for instance, David felt forsaken and aptly expressed his agony *to* God. He also acknowledged the holiness of God and that God is "enthroned in the praises of Israel." Moreover, since he was genuinely pouring out the pain of his heart *before* God through song (he was not complaining to people who could not offer any help), it was impossible for God not to *hear* and *answer* him. The psalmist, in the middle of the song, said: "You have answered me."[7] And from that moment on, the mood of the song changed. It became prophetic praise all the way to the end! The answer he received might have been "Yes, but not yet," but that was enough for an eruption of glorious praise!

This was how David could stay calm in the midst of perfect storms. The one whose anointed songs drove out oppressive spirits from his master, king Saul, knew how to use songs of worship to conquer depression that sought to drown him. The more David made this a habit, the more his awareness of God's presence while passing through death valleys.

The fact that the psalmists cried when in pain, but *also* tuned into God for strength makes their psalms very relatable. They have demonstrated unequivocally that no matter how desperate a situation may seem, an encounter with the glorious countenance of God awaits those who reach out to Him in worship.

Now, let us see how this principle of activating God's presence in worship plays out in the Levitical ministry of Asaph, a chief Levite in David's court. He wrote twelve psalms and, evidently, learned from David how to be open with God. His songs reveal the same practice of freely expressing heartfelt feelings before God, and a willingness to receive comfort from God.

What could happen if someone who knew the secret of activating God's presence through worship, chose not to do so? Or, what kind of situation is likely to challenge a worshipper's faith and trust in God? The seventy-third psalm has answers to these questions.

Asaph starts the psalm by acknowledging the goodness of God to Israel and to the pure in heart. But very quickly, he opens up about himself: "But as for me, my feet had almost stumbled; my steps had nearly slipped. For I was envious of the boastful, when I saw the *prosperity of the wicked*."

If there is one issue in life that many who profess faith find stressful, it would be the problems associated with provision. Finances, in one word. The necessity of money for survival and the fact that it is often in short supply, causes many to live in a constant state of despair. We worry about how to put food on the table, pay bills and save enough to enjoy the comforts of life. The situation is not helped by the knowledge that many who do not acknowledge God seem to have everything they want in life. What is the point of serving God when those who do not know him are prospering and I am not?

Asaph was open about his struggles in this area. He was burdened by it to the point of nearly turning away from God. "My feet had *almost* stumbled; my steps had *nearly* slipped," he confessed. By focusing on and envying what others had, Asaph began to despise what *he* had. Noticing that the wicked seem to only "increase in riches," he concluded that "surely I have cleansed my heart in vain, and washed my hands in innocence."

The longer Asaph protested the prosperity of the wicked, the deeper the anguish of his soul. He tried to work things out in his own mind and delayed setting his gaze away from his circumstances and on God. Depression will always prevail when we are fixated on the unfavourable conditions that gave rise to it in the first place. Focusing on his needy state and comparing himself with the wealth of others only fuelled his feelings of hopelessness.

Asaph knew he had to do what he had been taught to do; indeed, what he had done many times before. He could not harbour envy in his heart and be a faithful minister of God. He needed to refocus his mind on God.

> *When I thought how to understand this,*
>
> *It was too painful for me –*
>
> *Until I went into the sanctuary of God;*
>
> *Then I understood their end.*

Psalm 73:16,17

Asaph's pain persisted *until* he went into the sanctuary of God to worship. Once in the sanctuary, he could have an encounter with the presence and truths of God. He left that place of communion with a deeper level of *understanding* of what was going on, an understanding that he did not have prior to entering God's presence.

The stance he had *before* engaging God was one that questioned the righteousness and fairness of God. This position was like standing on quicksand and trying to reach for the heights. Asaph needed a firmer foundation underneath his feet; he needed a proper *stance*. He needed to understand his circumstances from God's superior perspective. He needed a peek into the bigger picture. And that is exactly what happened when he entered God's sanctuary. From that moment on, he experienced an upgrade in his understanding, and this completely changed his song. The lyrics of the song from that point on was all about the wisdom, plan and sovereignty of God.

Whom have I in heaven but You?

And there is none upon earth that I desire besides You.

My flesh and my heart fail;

But God is the strength of my heart and my portion forever.

For indeed, those who are far from You shall perish;

You have destroyed all those who desert You for harlotry.

But it is good for me to draw near to God;

I have put my trust in the Lord God,

That I may declare all Your works.

Psalm 73:25-28

I can testify that "it is good for me to draw near to God" during times of despair. When the mood is low because of adverse circumstances, one may not feel drawn to prayer or worship; melodies of the heart that God loves to hear may seemingly disappear. Yet, we can *find* a way to draw near to God. What helped me over the years was a commitment to writing my prayers to God, knowing that He read them. I kept journals of my thoughts and supplications, and drew near to God in this way. I knew that He did not mind "reading" my complaints; what was more important was that I was connecting with and pouring my heart to Him.

Before long, I began to appreciate that God was truly mindful of me in spite of my situation. I discovered that He wanted to work *in* me and not just *for* me. I understood that a change of *outer circumstances* without a change of *inner perspectives* would not yield lasting dividends. I knew I had to embrace *inner transformation* and wait patiently, sometimes painfully, for *outer transformation*.

Ultimately, change within will lead to a change without. Wisdom that flows from the heart's fountain will, in time, work wonders no matter the external mountain. Knowing these truths have kept me in spite of how I felt. They have become an anchor to the soul, connecting me to the ever-abiding presence of the Almighty.

#GODISMINDFULOFYOU

Oh the glory of God's presence! Welcome to awesome glory that rests upon the temple of your heart! The sanctuary of the Lord is not a building or a mountain; it is your heart connected to His; it is hearts connected with Him in the centre. Outside of this place, there might be inequality, unfairness and injustice, but in the presence of His sovereignty, there is righteousness, mercy and truth. Come, therefore, and behold the beauty of the Lord. He shall make all things new and wipe away your every tear. You do not need to worry about your life. He cares for you more than the lilies of the field and the birds of the air. Those who trust in the Lord will never be put to shame. They will find help in His presence, an intervention that will prove yet again that He is. God will never leave you nor forsake you. As you worship from this place of understanding, you will experience breakthrough after breakthrough, within and without. The Lord is mindful of you. Draw near unto Him and He will draw near unto you.

PRACTICAL TIPS

◆ *Be open about your pain and daily struggles. Share them with God as you worship. Write a song. Write to God in your journal.*

◆ *Worship instead of worry. Interrupt the troubled silence within you with worship songs that exalt God over circumstances. As you worship, make a note of any insight and understanding God places in your heart, including ideas for generating finance.*

◆ *Maintain an active expectation of the intervention of God's presence. Allow yourself to move into prophetic praise and declaration. Worship freely with other worshippers.*

OCEANS (WHERE FEET MAY FAIL)

You call me out upon the waters
The great unknown where feet may fail
And there I find You in the mystery
In oceans deep my faith will stand

I will call upon Your Name
And keep my eyes above the waves
When oceans rise
My soul will rest in Your embrace
For I am Yours and You are mine

Your grace abounds in deepest waters
Your sovereign hand will be my guide
Where feet may fail and fear surrounds me
You've never failed and You won't start now

Bridge

Spirit lead me where my trust is without borders
Let me walk upon the waters
Wherever You would call me
Take me deeper than my feet could ever wander
And my faith will be made stronger
In the presence of my Saviour

I will call upon Your Name
Keep my eyes above the waves
My soul will rest in Your embrace
I am Yours and You are mine

Words and Music by Matt Crocker,
Joel Houston & Salomon Lightelm

Copyright © by Hillsong United

FINAL WORD

FREE INDEED!
(John 8:31-36)

❧

As we have seen over and over again, God is mindful of all His children, especially those who are going through seasons of oppression in their minds. God cares about your spirit, soul and body. He cares about the state of your mind. He wants you to live free of depression. He wants you set apart for Him through and through. For this purpose, He will go out of His way to visit you. It is for this same reason, I believe, you have read this book — to experience the visitation of God within you, an encounter with His presence and truth.

> *What is man that You are mindful of him,*
> *And the son of man that You visit him?*
> **Psalm 8:4**

Every story in this book, beginning from mine, reveals a God who takes the initiative to reach out to the downcast in soul. He seeks out the lost and restores the afflicted to wholeness. He does this because He cares.

In the final chapter, however, the short exposition of the psalmists' experiences, we learn that we should also take the initiative to seek God during times of despair. If we *know* and *trust* God, we should enter His sanctuary with thanksgiving, praise and worship. Chains of depression break when we enter the presence of God. Asaph said, "It is good for me to draw near to God." When we draw near to Him, He draws near to us. And we can draw near to Him because He, in Christ, first drew near to us.

Now, when Jesus drew near to the paralysed man at the pool of Bethesda (story in chapter four), the authority of His instruction - *"Rise, take up your bed and walk"* - was enough to deliver the man from thirty-eight years of bondage. The man broke free of the stranglehold of depression and negative thinking in an instant. What a powerful impact of the visit of Christ that day!

However, Jesus considered it necessary to visit the man *again*. He wanted to make sure his healing lasted for as long as he lived. After seeking the man amongst the crowd, *"Jesus found him in the temple, and said to him, 'See, you have been made well. Sin no more, lest a worse thing come upon you.'"* This *second encounter* was significant.

The thought that is likely to immediately come to our minds is that the man's sins were responsible for his condition in the first place; and that he had to maintain his freedom by remaining sinless. Well, we are not privy to his background and history. The full essence of this instruction was a personal matter for the man. He would have known what Jesus meant by those words; he knew his own past mistakes, the effects of which he was now free. These could be, for instance, the negative thoughts that he clung unto, or the tendency to reject personal responsibility and blame others instead. Whatever they were, he knew exactly what Jesus meant.

But Jesus was not placing a burden on him to strive for perfection in his own strength, or prevent a relapse through the exercise of his will. Far from it. The power to live free of his errors and walk in wholeness was in the very words of that instruction: "Sin no more." The statement was not a burden, but an impartation of a sense of responsibility backed by Christ's authority. This was Grace to live in freedom and enjoy wholeness; Grace that should not be taken for granted. Hence the statement, "lest a worse thing come upon you."

I know my own story. You know yours. They may contain "sins" of various kinds, but these have not prevented Jesus from reaching out to us with His love, presence and truth. "Sins" do not refer only to bad things that we do; it also refers the good things that we know to that we fail to do (James 4:17). Now that we are set free, we should walk in the authority of Christ's words and "sin no more." This is Grace in all its authenticity!

Jesus communicated this truth in another way:

"Jesus said to those Jews who believed Him, 'If you abide in My word, you are My disciples indeed. And you shall know the truth, and the truth shall make you free… Therefore if the Son makes you free, you shall be free indeed."

John 8:31-32,36

Restating these words in the light of its context, Jesus was saying, "When you encounter the Son (the presence of Jesus) and His truth (which essentially are one), you will become free, and as you walk in the Son and in His truth, you shall be free indeed."

As you delight yourself in the Lord, giving yourself to worshipping in His presence; as you draw near to God in devotion and service; as you walk in the truths you have come to know, you shall be free indeed!

There is just *one more* thing to say about freedom that lasts. After the man who was once bound received the authority from Christ to walk in freedom, "The man departed and told the Jews that it was Jesus who had made him well." He went to spread the news about Jesus.

After the one who was once an outcast was freed from bondage, "he departed and began to proclaim in Decapolis all that Jesus had done for him; and all marveled."

After the woman at the well encountered Jesus and was freed from dejection, she ran to the city to proclaim the good news about Jesus.

After Peter was freed from self-reliance and self-doubt, he embraced the commission to feed Jesus' flock.

After Cleopas and his friend encountered Jesus and experienced a lifting out of despair, they "rose up that very hour and returned to Jerusalem" to share the good news about the risen Christ.

After Asaph encountered the presence and truth of God in the sanctuary, he resolved to declare God's works abroad.

Now that you have encountered the God who cares deeply for you and experienced freedom from oppression, you should share your testimony with others. Let them know that Jesus truly cares. This would be the evidence that you are free indeed.

This is why I wrote this book. I am free indeed!

#GODISMINDFULOFYOU

Here are some suggestions for spreading the good news of Jesus and His power to set free:

- Write a Facebook post and share your story.
- Send a Tweet and share your story.
- Share your story on social media platforms you use.
- Send a post to your WhatsApp broadcast list and recommend this book.
- Write a review of this book on Amazon.
- Recommend the book to someone who might be struggling with depression.
- Share a testimony in your small group.
- Study and share the principles of this book with others (feed my lambs).
- Share your story no matter your backstory!

"Therefore if the Son makes you free,
you shall be free indeed!"

ACKNOWLEDGEMENTS

I am grateful to God for the inspiration to write this book and the freedom to share my story. Father, you are faithful.

Many thanks to my spiritual father, Dr. Hugh Osgood, for his invaluable input into sections of this book. Special thanks, also, to Rev. Kayode Tadese, who also gave helpful feedback.

Thanks also to everyone who read and endorsed the work. My friends around the world did a good job in critiquing the covers. Thanks to my designer, Agnesa, who created the stir!

Thanks to my scribal community, *The Scribal Hub*, for their loyal support and encouragement.

Finally, thanks to my family: to my dear wife, Linda, for persevering through years of famine; to my children, Destiny, Daniel and David, for showing unconditional love for their daddy. *I love you all, deeply.*

REFERENCES

FIRST WORD

1. Emmanuel, T. (2010), *The Shift of a Lifetime*, Sophos Books, London.

2. WHO (2001), *World Health Report*. Available at: <https://www.who.int/news-room/detail/28-09-2001-the-world-health-report-2001-mental-disorders-affect-one-in-four-people> (accessed: 13 June 2020).

THE COMING MINDEMIC

1. Schizophrenia is a mental health condition that impacts the ability of a person to control their thoughts and sometimes their actions. It can result in hallucinations, delusions, withdrawal from social activities and others effects. (www.rethink.org).

2. In very simplistic terms, situational depression is caused by circumstantial triggers that result in momentary or prolonged seasons of despair; while clinical depression, a more severe form of depression, could be the result of chemical imbalances, genetic factors or untreated situational depression (www.medicalnewstoday.com).

3. Emmanuel, T. (2010), *The Shift of a Lifetime*, Sophos Books, London.

THE GOD WHO CARES

1. Jonah 1:5
2. Mark 4:38
3. Matthew 27:46
4. 1 Peter 5:7

BEYOND THE STORM

1. Mark 4:35
2. Mark 5:15
3. Mark 5:20

GIVE ME A DRINK

1. John 4:1-3
2. John 4:4
3. Matthew 9:10-13; Luke 7:34, 15:2
4. The Lord gave me insight into this precious woman's backstory. Get a copy of my book, *The Greatest Well-digger in the World* for details.

WOULD YOU BE MADE WHOLE?

1. Proverbs 23:7

DO YOU LOVE ME?

1. See Genesis 32:22-32
2. See Luke 5:1-11
3. Matthew 14:22-33
4. Matthew 26:31-34

5.   Matthew 26:69-75

6.   Romans 7:24

7.   Luke 22:31-32

ON THE EMMAUS ROAD

1.   1 John 5:14-15

2.   2 Corinthians 1:20

3.   Proverbs 13:12

OUT OF THE CAVE

1.   1 Kings 18:20-40

2.   1 Kings 18:1,41-44

3.   1 Corinthians 10:12

4.   1 Samuel 17:44-47

5.   Exodus 33:19-23

6.   1 Kings 18:7-16

ENTER THE SANCTUARY

1.   Psalm 16:11

2.   John 8:32

3.   Isaiah 61:3

4.   1 Samuel 18:10

5.   Psalm 22:1

6.   Psalm 22:27-29

7.   Psalm 22:21

ALSO BY TOKUNBO EMMANUEL

The Greatest Well-digger in the World
The Secret of Abraham
The Wells of Isaac
The Destiny of Jacob
The Shift of a Lifetime
Miracle Shift
The Faith Clinic Revival
Run, Church Run!
The Mandate of Paul
And many more!

For these and other books by Tokunbo Emmanuel,
visit his page on Amazon or go to:

www.booksbytoks.com